BORN AGAIN - THE MAN THEY COULDN'T KILL

To Naomi
Every Blessing
Jim Stewart
HEBS 13 v 2

Born Again - The Man They Couldn't Kill

Jim Stewart

Christian Year Publications

ISBN-13: 978 1 872734 41 5

Copyright © 2014 by Christian Year Publications

All rights reserved. No part of this publication may be reproduced, stored in a retrievable system, or transmitted in any form or by any other means – electronic, mechanical, photocopy, recording or otherwise – without prior permission of the copyright owner.

Typeset by John Ritchie Ltd., Kilmarnock
Printed by Bell & Bain Ltd., Glasgow

ILLUSTRATED BY GEORGIA COLLINS

Georgia is a student of Friends' School, Lisburn, County Antrim, where she is studying Art & Design, English and Moving Image Arts and hopes to pursue a career in Graphic Design and Illustration.

>ggcollins195@hotmail.co.uk

The author can be contacted for speaking engagements at:

j.stewart672@btinternet.com

DEDICATION

SAMUEL FISHER
1939 - 2013

I dedicate this book to the memory of my dear friend and former colleague, Big Sam. I greatly valued his true friendship, support and his wise counsel over many years and I recall with fondness our time together. Most of the contents of this book had been discussed with Sam on many occasions. Sam Fisher, a true gentleman and a true friend who sadly lost his battle with cancer in August 2013. May his memory live on through this book. He will be sadly missed but fondly remembered by all who knew and loved him.

Contents

Chapter 1: Born Again 11
Chapter 2: Sunday School Teacher 15
Chapter 3: Part-time Job 17
Chapter 4: Attempted Murder 27
Chapter 5: Sandy Row Murder 32
Chapter 6: The Big Decision 37
Chapter 7: Shantallow - Londonderry 40
Chapter 8: Drunken Nights 43
Chapter 9: Divine Protection 46
Chapter 10: Angels Watching Over Me 49
Chapter 11: The Only Man I Couldn't Kill 52
Chapter 12: Covert Operations 55
Chapter 13: Suffer Little Children 57
Chapter 14: Medical Discharge 61
Chapter 15: Stanley Close 63
Chapter 16: My Son James 68
Chapter 17: Stranger: Angel or Messenger 72
Chapter 18: Two Hours to Live 76
Chapter 19: Testing Times - Adele 80
Chapter 20: James - Today 82
Chapter 21: Why Me Lord? 83

CHAPTER 1

Born Again

The year 1955 was memorable for many different reasons, did you know that in 1955 Winston Churchill resigned as Prime Minister of Britain. The Independent Television Authority (ITA) was launched and, that Albert Einstein died aged seventy six. The famous Hollywood actor James Dean was killed in a car crash, Ruth Ellis was hanged in London for killing her lover and, the country had been held in the grip of a big freeze that year, also the Guinness book of world records was first published. Oh yes of course one other memorable event worthy of note records the birth of one James Stewart at the Jubilee Maternity Hospital in Belfast. While this information pales into insignificance in comparison with other world events it was, none the less memorable for me, and for my family. The first born into a family of three boys and raised in the Village area of Belfast's Donegall Road where I would enjoy an uneventful childhood.

BELFAST CITY MISSION
I had a normal Christian up-bringing and I was fortunate that my mother had sent me along to Sunday School, just as soon as I could walk. Belfast in the 1950's had a church or mission hall on almost every street corner, much like today. I was sent along to the Belfast City Mission hall in Kilburn Street just off the Donegall Road, in Belfast. It was then, and still is today, a very small wooden hall on the street corner located within a very tight knit working class community. I have fond memories of the old wooden building with its hard wooden benches, the hand painted scripture verse above the platform and the smell of bleach from its immaculately scrubbed wooden floors. This was a place I really loved, and where I wanted to spend time.

I was faithfully sent along to the Sunday School every Sunday afternoon where, I first heard those wonderful bible stories about the life of Jesus. As we gathered in the wee hall every Sunday we would sing choruses, learn our memory verses and be taught how to pray. I would sit captivated while my Sunday School teacher told us those wonderful stories which were to have such a huge impact on my young life, at that time and throughout my entire life.

My earliest memory is of the missionary Mr. Cassidy. There was also Bobby Beattie, Derek Finley and his wife Ruby, Ethel McAllistar my old Sunday school teacher, Lily McAuley, Thelma Crowthers, Margaret Wilkinson, and Hessie Beattie to name but a few, they were all faithful and dedicated Sunday school teachers and all, Godly men and women. I am grateful to God for every one of them, for their faithfulness and dedication in pointing me in the direction of Jesus. Looking back over the years even with changes in missionary personnel which saw Mr. Cassidy replaced by Mr. Billy Cooke who later went on to become the Secretary of the Belfast City Mission. Mr. Cooke was then replaced by David Campbell who was later replaced by Robin Fairbairn. However, my abiding memory is that all these men were faithful and fearless preachers of the gospel of Jesus Christ. Sadly in some of our churches today this is not the case, for in many of our churches, it seems that in an age of political correctness gone mad some so called ministers of the gospel are afraid to preach that simple, but true, gospel message that warns us that we are all born as hell deserving sinners, but for the sacrifice of the Lord Jesus Christ on the cross at Calvary for our salvation. It seems that they are afraid of offending anyone or rocking the boat, to such an extent that they have turned people away from God, by turning their back on the gospel, and they seem indifferent and content in seeing souls being lost to a Christ-less eternity. We as Christians have a duty to go into all the world and preach the gospel, to be faithful and true ambassadors of Christ, and the only way we can achieve this, is to speak the truth in these dark days of apostasy. Remember the bible teaches us, that the truth will set you free. I am grateful to God for

Born Again

the Belfast City Mission who have never compromised on preaching the true gospel message. Today they continue to work in the working class areas of Belfast reaching out from generation to generation and proclaiming the good news of that gospel and continue to be a blessing to many people.

From a very early age, and as a result of this faithful preaching, I became aware that I had indeed been born a sinner just like everyone else and, that I needed to ask the Lord Jesus Christ into my heart. The thought of being a lost sinner troubled me greatly for a very long time. Despite this knowledge, I had not yet experienced the working of God's Holy Spirit in my life to convict me of my sin. Although, I knew nothing of the Holy Spirit at that time.

However, on a cold winter's night in 1962, at the age of seven, while at the Monday night children's meeting in Kilburn Street, Belfast City Mission hall, I fell under conviction of my sin and, I was greatly upset. So, at the end of the meeting I stayed behind to speak with my Sunday school teacher, Ethel McAllister. After we had spoken for a short time she brought me to the front of the little mission hall and set me down on the old wooden bench on the left hand side of the hall. As we spoke my heart was very heavy with a burden that would not go away, and with fear and trembling, I asked the Lord Jesus Christ to come into my heart with a simple child like prayer. Only then was my burden lifted, my sins were forgiven and I was set free. Immediately I felt at peace, and I was filled with a joy and unbelievable happiness as if a heavy load had been lifted off my mind. I remember running all the way home to tell my mother that I had become a Christian, much to her delight. The Belfast City Mission is very precious to me, and it holds a very special place in my heart, and always will.

This was the first Divine working of God's Holy Spirit in my young life, but it would certainly not be the last. I will go on and tell you more of my experiences and divine interventions in my life during the years that followed my conversion, which is now over fifty years ago.

Born Again - The Man They Couldn't Kill

JESUS ANSWERED AND SAID UNTO HIM, VERILY, VERILY, I SAY UNTO THEE, EXCEPT A MAN BE BORN AGAIN, HE CANNOT SEE THE KINGDOM OF GOD.

JOHN 3v3 KJV

Belfast City Mission Hall, Kilburn Street.

Harvest Service, Kilburn Street Mission Hall, Belfast, 2002.

CHAPTER 2

Sunday School Teacher

After my conversion I continued to walk with the Lord, and was full of enthusiasm and a new found sense of happiness that I had never known before. Over the years that followed my conversion, I continued attending Sunday school, along with the Monday night meeting, the Wednesday night youth club, on Thursday night I attended the Boys Brigade at Donegall Road Methodist church, the 38th Belfast company, and on Friday night I attended the Christian endeavour. So almost every night I was involved with the church in some way and there was nowhere else I would rather be than in the house of God.

As I continued to mature in my Christian faith I was asked to become a Sunday school teacher in Kilburn Street, City Mission hall at the tender age of fifteen. I really enjoyed teaching Sunday school and, as I prepared for my lessons I was also able to learn more about the Lord Jesus and His ministry, His miracles, and all those wonderful Bible stories which I would then be able to relate to the kids in my Sunday school class. I got to know each child personally and, I was able to build up great relationships with all of them. While they were all basically good kids, there was of course the odd one who would be more of a challenge than the others, I am sure you know the type, rowdy, talkative and disruptive, so as a result I was to learn great patience and perseverance which would prove to be worth all the extra effort I put in, as I would find out much later in life, much to my amazement. Remember that seed sown, is seed planted, and if it had no impact at that time, it may well have impact later on in life.

Teaching Sunday school was a most enjoyable and rewarding time in my life and it gave me a real passion for Sunday school work, which I still have to this day.

TRAIN UP A CHILD IN THE WAY HE SHOULD GO, AND WHEN HE IS OLD, HE WILL NOT DEPART FROM IT.

PROVERBS 22 v 6 KJV

CHAPTER 3

Part-time Job

By now at the age of fifteen, I was attending Fane Street secondary school just a short walk away from my home. I have mixed feelings about my time at school, while I was relatively happy there most of the time, there were moments of discontent with the odd teacher I didn't like, or the usual, but extremely annoying bullies or, as they liked to be known, the "hard men" of the school. There was a certain element at the school who would later become involved in loyalist paramilitary activity, and as I look back this was inevitable given the nature of the political unrest in the country at that time.

At that time my only source of income was from my weekly paper round as I worked for Curleys newsagent shop in Broadway. By now I had outgrown my paper round and was looking for a part-time job which would help supplement my pocket money. I had now developed an interest in music and clothes and the usual things with teenage appeal. Therefore I decided to take a part-time job in the local Maxol petrol station in Tates Avenue, Belfast, just a few hundred yards from my home. In those days no one filled their own cars with petrol, that was the job of the petrol pump attendant. My responsibilities also extended to sales in the shop, monitoring the money coming into the shop and, when a certain amount of money had been collected, it was then placed inside a canister and dropped into an underground safe. At the beginning and end of my shift, I would take the pump readings and I hoped that they would all tally up before closing time. This was all straight forward enough, easy and uncomplicated, however, little did I know that a dark cloud would descend and change my life greatly.

I was only working two nights each week, and on Saturday I would work a full day. I was enjoying this work and I knew most of the customers coming in and out of the shop, as most of them lived in the local area. At this time in the early seventies, Northern Ireland was now in the grip of what has become known as "The Troubles". Terrorist activity was an everyday occurrence, but for me, it was only something to be seen on T.V. or when it would be reported in the newspapers. I had only ever observed the Troubles from a distance when I happened to pass by a bombed out shop or building in the city centre, making me see the devastation first hand. At no time did I ever imagine that one day, I would be caught up in the troubles, or that the troubles would come to my own front door.

ARMED ROBBERY

One evening, when I was working in the petrol station, a well known thug walked into the shop. I knew him well as we had both been in the same class at primary school and he was now attending the same secondary school as me, although not in the same class. This particular individual was someone I had always avoided, as he was a well known trouble maker, a bully and someone who was always fighting. He was bad news, both inside and outside school. This person shall remain nameless for obvious reasons, but I will refer to him as "Spud" for the purposes of this book, (this name does not remotely relate to his real name or his true identity). One day, while I was working in the petrol station, there was an uneasy atmosphere as I saw Spud from a short distance away. He walked across the forecourt and entered the shop. As I waited for him to make a purchase, he turned to me with a smirk on his face, and then he produced a handgun from the waistband of his trousers, which he thrust into my stomach, followed by the words, " this is a robbery, give me all the money or I'll shoot you ". My heart started pounding with a fear I had never known before. I hoped this was just a joke, but when he grabbed me by the throat and forced me to the ground I knew that he meant business and that this was for real. I opened the till, and told him to take whatever he wanted. I watched in horror as his grubby little hand

Part-time Job

reached across me and into the till, which he then emptied of all the money. There was not a lot of money in the till as we had been told to count it regularly and place it in the safe, leaving only enough for change. Spud was not happy with the small amount of money he had taken, so he shouted at me, "Where's the rest of the money before I shoot you?" I tried to explain to him that the rest of the money was placed in a safe under the ground, but he did not believe me. Again he became violent, pushing me to the floor and putting the gun to my head, threatening to shoot me. I pleaded with him to go before anyone came in and he was caught. He eventually left, but before he walked out the door he turned back to me and said " If you tell the cops it was me you're dead. Remember I know where you live so I'll come back and shoot you, your Ma and Da and your brothers. "I was left petrified and in deep shock, not knowing what to do; I was so confused. Spud had come into the petrol station in broad daylight, not wearing a mask and armed with what seemed to me to be a great big handgun, threatening to kill me if I did not co-operate. I did not even have time to pray, in fact I was unable to pray after he had gone, such was my shock at what had just happened.

Needless to say, the police were called eventually and after spending some time examining the scene, I was taken to Lisburn Road police station to make a statement. So when I told them exactly what had happened I deliberately gave them no information that could remotely relate to Spud, for fear of the consequences. This was the start of many sleepless nights which filled me with fear and a reluctance to return to the petrol station to work, after all it was only for a pittance of pocket money and certainly not worth getting killed for. I managed to convince myself that this was a one off, perhaps a spur of the moment thing, and that I may never see him again. However, I did go back to work, despite being fearful of Spud's return. I thought he could not be stupid enough to return to commit another robbery so soon after the first one. I hoped that he may have thought the police would be watching the place awaiting his return, but still, I knew he was a nut case and that he could just as easily return to the scene of the crime given that he was a bit thick. I really did not have long to wait, for a few days later the door of the shop opened and there was Spud. He asked me what I had told the police and I quickly informed him, that I told them nothing. I knew the same thing was about to happen again, and of course it did. Out came the gun, I opened the till, and he helped himself to the money, although this time it was much more civilised, with no repeat of the violence I had previously experienced. Before leaving the premises, he reminded me to say nothing or else I was a dead man.

Over a period of three weeks Spud had robbed the petrol station seven times, but, only on the occasions when I was working. I knew that it was only a matter of time until the police would suspect me of being involved in the robberies with Spud, and I feared that I might be arrested and forced to tell them the truth. This could have had serious repercussions for me, and my family. I had no option but to play along with Spud and continue telling the police lies in order to protect us. I think it was at this point I really started to fear for my life. I was asked by police to provide a photo-fit likeness of the suspect which I had agreed to do. However, the description I gave to police was completely imaginary and in no way resembled Spud in any shape or form, it was in fact a completely false description. I did not even stop to consider that the information I had now provided to the police may look like some innocent person that I could get into trouble, such was my fear. Not to mention my conscience, after all here I was, a Christian, and I was telling the police a pack of lies to save my own skin. This lay heavily on my mind and contributed to many more sleepless nights.

THE SET-UP
By now Spud was coming to the petrol station at will, and just helping himself to the money in the till, but on this one occasion he turned to me and offered me money to keep my mouth shut. I refused, telling him I did not want any part of it, which seemed to please him, as I knew he surely had sensed my fear. I was opening the petrol station up one Saturday morning to start an eight hour shift. I had just turned the key in the door when, from out of nowhere Spud appeared in the

doorway and pushed me inside the shop. I noticed blood on his right hand which he had seen me looking at, and he then proudly announced that he had carried out another armed robbery the night before at the Balmoral petrol station on the Lisburn Road, Belfast. He boasted that the manager got a bit brave and refused to co-operate with him so " I just beat him with the gun until he gave me the money, that's how I cut my hand, so don't you get brave or the same thing will happen to you". Then he announced that he was going into the toilets to wash the blood from his hand and that I should have all the money ready for him when he returned from the toilets. I explained to him that I had no money except for the float which I used for change to open the shop, and that I had not even served one customer yet, so there was no money available other than my twelve pounds float. On his return from the toilet he told me to collect all the money and not to put any of it into the safe. I was to keep all the money for him as he would be back later to collect it at around 11am. As he turned to walk away he stopped momentarily and came back to tell me, that on his return he was going to break my nose. When I asked why he would do such a thing he replied, "To make this look real so that the police would not suspect me of being involved." He then turned and walked away with the gun stuck down the front of his jeans.

I was terrified and I started praying that God would help me to end this nightmare. God spoke clearly to me in my time of need and gave me the courage to make the decision that enough was enough. So I decided that I would collect all the money and not place any of it in the safe. Instead I would collect all the bank notes and record all the serial numbers which I would then hand to the police before the next robbery and hopefully they would be able to arrest Spud and bring this nightmare to an end. I nervously scribbled down the serial numbers of all the bank notes I had collected that morning. I rang the detectives at Lisburn Road CID where I spoke to the detective in charge of the case, Detective Sergeant Gordon Orr and I explained to him my plan. I asked him to come to the petrol station and pretend to be a customer coming in for petrol. When he would come into the shop to pay for his petrol, I would slip him the serial numbers that I had already recorded on a rough piece of paper. This all went according to plan and he told me that they would be sitting in an unmarked police car waiting for the robbery to take place. I felt a sense of relief as well as impending doom, hoping that all would go well, and that I would not get hurt. All I really wanted now was for Spud to be caught red handed. About an hour later I saw Spud make his approach but, for the first time he was accompanied by another older male person who was dressed in combat gear and who looked really menacing. I recognised this person as someone from the local area. Spud came in and without a word I immediately handed him the money. Not satisfied with that he turned to me and said," Right we are going to beat you up and break your nose now." I protested and pleaded with him that I had done everything he had asked of me, so just leave me alone and take the money and go. The man accompanying him said "Come on leave it," then both men left the shop and walked across the road into Benburb Street where they disappeared up an entry and out of site. As I waited for police to arrive I expected a flurry of activity or even a gun battle to take place. There was nothing, just complete silence. Nothing happened, there was no movement, no sirens or flashing lights, no armed police officers in hot pursuit and so I had no idea if Spud had been apprehended, or if he had escaped and was now on his way back to shoot me, I just did not know. By now fear had set in and I had become very anxious. I found it hard to handle the uncertainty and I fully expected Spud to return and shoot me at any moment. As I waited for his return I tried to plan an escape route. This seemed futile as there was only one door in and one door out of the shop and a lot of open ground in between where I could easily have been picked off.

So I continued working and as the minutes turned into hours, eventually I received a phone call from the police to say that Spud had been arrested, and that he had thrown a gun over a yard wall which was later recovered by police in a follow up search, the gun turned out to be a replica. Spud was now in police custody and I was assured that I would be safe and I had nothing to worry about. However, these words

Part-time Job

rang hollow as I did not feel safe at all. Police called to my home later that night to record a statement and they were full of praise for the courageous stand that I had taken. But I was informed that I might need to appear in court to give evidence against Spud, should he decide to plead not guilty. That was a long way off and the police said that they would make sure that nothing would happen to me. What I was feeling now was relief but also fear of what might happen in the future for I knew Spud had both friends and family connected to the para-militaries and that they would not let this go without some sort of retaliation. By now I was at my wits end, afraid to leave the house and when I did manage to leave the house I was always looking over my shoulder for some sort of revenge attack.

THE FIRST ATTACK

Several months had now gone by without incident but I had been told indirectly by the local para-militaries that I was a marked man. One afternoon I had gone to the nearby shops for my mother. When I came out of the local fruit shop which was on the corner of Tates Avenue, I became aware of a blue coloured Ford Anglia car with a white roof moving down the street very slowly with at least three people on board. I

*The Village Fruit Shop, Tate's Avenue, Belfast.
Scene of gun attack.*

became very suspicious and when I observed the front seat passenger's window come down slowly, I saw something coming out of the window. Fearing for my life I ran as fast as my legs could carry me as the car began to follow me at speed. Then at the junction of Tates Avenue and Ebor Street shots rang out followed by shouting. The car took off at high speed along Tates Avenue in the direction of Donegall Avenue. I realized then I had just survived an assassination attempt on my life. I was later informed by police I had been the intended target of local para-militaries for putting Spud in jail, and that my life was now in extreme danger. I remember that my parents and some family friends went to see the local godfathers to seek assurances that nothing would happen to me, but to no avail. They were told that this powerful group had nothing to do with the recent attempt on my life and they could offer no assurances for my safety. They denied all knowledge of any involvement in the gun attack.

I lived in fear for the months which followed, and despite all the assurances I got from the police that I would be safe, I remained terrified. Some time later the police called at my house and served me with a summons to appear at Crumlin Road courthouse to give evidence against Spud. Leading up to the court case I had prayed like I had never prayed before that I would not have to go to court and give evidence. The police informed me the day before the case was due to be heard, Spud was pleading not guilty, and I would now be required to attend court to give my evidence in person. On the day of the court case I left home dressed in my Sunday best after telling my parents I was going to meet the police who would take me to the court and bring me home again. In fact I did a runner. I was extremely fearful so I walked the several miles from my home to Shaw's Bridge. There I walked along the banks of the River Lagan enjoying the peace and tranquillity of the beautiful gardens alongside the river. There were no mobile phones in those days and so no one could get in touch with me. I walked along the River Lagan and prayed that God would prevent me from having to go to court and give evidence. As I walked along the banks of the River Lagan the words of a well known hymn came into my mind and as I started singing I found real peace and comfort for the first time in a long time, as I sang these words:

I COME TO THE GARDEN ALONE
WHILE THE DEW IS STILL ON THE ROSES
AND THE VOICE I HEAR FALLING ON MY EAR
THE SON OF GOD DISCLOSES

HE SPEAKS AND THE SOUND OF HIS VOICE
IS SO SWEET THE BIRDS HUSH THEIR SINGING
AND THE MELODY THAT HE GAVE TO ME
WITHIN MY HEART IS RINGING

I'D STAYED IN THE GARDEN WITH HIM
THOUGH THE NIGHT AROUND ME BE FALLING
BUT HE BIDS ME GO THROUGH THE VOICE OF WOE
HIS VOICE TO ME IS CALLING

CHORUS.
AND HE WALKS WITH ME AND HE TALKS WITH ME
AND HE TELLS ME I AM HIS OWN
AND THE JOY WE SHARE AS WE TARRY THERE
NONE OTHER HAS EVER KNOWN

Shaw's Bridge, River Lagan.

When I returned home that night I was greeted by my mother who asked me where I had been since the police had been looking for me to tell me the good news. Spud had pleaded guilty and I was no longer needed at court, it was all over. I was overjoyed that my prayer had been answered and as I gave thanks to God, I remembered the words of the hymn I had sung a short time earlier and which has become one of my favourite hymns of all time. Spud was sentenced to five years in the Maze Prison. At last this menace had been removed from society.

THOU WILT KEEP HIM IN PERFECT PEACE, WHOSE MIND IS STAYED ON THEE: BECAUSE HE TRUSTETH IN THEE.

ISAIAH 26v3 KJV

CHAPTER 4

Attempted Murder

In 1976 I decided to join the part-time reserve of the Royal Ulster Constabulary. This was at the start of the Northern Ireland troubles and it was a very volatile and dangerous time for all serving members of the security forces. There was a constant threat from both republican and loyalist terror groupings. As a result I now found myself armed with a gun, a personal protection weapon which had to be carried on and off duty and at all times because of the threat from the IRA who were now hell bent on killing soft targets such as, police officers and part time UDR soldiers. This threat would continue throughout my entire police service. After my initial training I was stationed at Donegal Pass police station in Belfast, convenient to the city centre, and one of the busiest police stations in the province. The police station was located just over one mile from my family home and, was also responsible for policing the Village area where I lived with my parents and two younger brothers. It did not take long for the locals in the area to find out that I was now a part time policeman. This created more hatred and resentment towards both me and my family from the local gangsters and para-militaries alike. However, we enjoyed great support from our friends and neighbours and of course all decent law abiding citizens who gave their full support to the rule of law and order and to all members of the security forces.

During the annual "twelfth of July celebrations I was on duty on the eleventh night, the eve before the twelfth" I had been sent into my own area of the village, only a matter of yards from my home to help police the bonfires, our role was to protect property and to deal with any public disorder if, and when it occurred. While some of the smaller bonfires were lit early to facilitate the younger children, the main bonfire and the largest one was always set alight at midnight and was always located at the junction of Ebor Street and Broadway. Crowds would gather to have street parties and house parties in the hours before the highlight of the evening the big bonfire. Inevitably the majority of onlookers would be under the influence of alcohol, with many in high spirits due to the influence of alcohol, and others spoiling for a good fight. The enormous bonfire, comprising mostly of railway sleepers acquired from the local railway line was towering

A typical Bonfire in the Village Area of South Belfast.

Attempted Murder

over the little terraced houses while those houses closest to the fire were always at the risk of catching fire from blowing heat, flames and burning embers. Our task was to monitor the situation and contact the fire service if we thought they were needed. This was quite normal in those days and for as long as I could remember since my childhood days growing up in the area and spending most of my summer holidays collecting wood for the bonfires year after year and it still remains a big part of our local tradition today.

Just before midnight as the crowds began to gather I was standing in uniform with another colleague in Broadway,

Children's Bonfire, Ebor Street, Belfast.

29

only a few yards away from the bonfire site. I had my back against a wall when, as if from nowhere a pint glass was thrown at me, smashing against the wall and narrowly missing my head. I saw a person running away and assumed that they had thrown the glass so, instinctively I gave chase following him into one of the many side streets. I observed him running into an entry behind the shops between Ebor Street and Moltke Street which were in complete darkness.

A NARROW ESCAPE
I was aware that a car had stopped, somewhat abruptly just in front of me and, narrowly missed hitting me. Suddenly a strong arm reached out and grabbed me, pulling me into the back seat of a police car. Then a loud instruction was shouted out to the driver to "get out of here fast". While in the police car and, after everyone had caught their breath the sergeant informed me that they had received a tip off that I was going to be shot. It was explained that after a meeting in a flat above the shops in Broadway from where I was spotted that two guns had been handed over by the para-militaries with instructions to lure me into a trap behind the shops, where I would be shot. This apparently was to be carried out by Spuds friends. I was then driven away at high speed back to Donegall Pass police station where I was debriefed by senior police officers before being escorted back to my home some time later. There was a static police presence placed outside my home that night.

Delighted as I was for this intervention, I now wanted to know the exact details behind this so called tip off and how the police knew where and when they needed to be at precisely the right time in order to prevent my death. The answer to my questions suggested that police at Belfast regional control had received an anonymous telephone call giving the exact details of the entire incident, from the throwing of the glass, the direction that I would be running and the entry where I was going to be shot. The message was then allegedly conveyed through Belfast Regional Control direct to a mobile police unit already on the ground and driving towards my location at the exact time of the transmission and was only a few seconds away. The driver had to brake to avoid hitting me and within an instant I was transported to safety, as if in the blinking of an eye.

DIVINE PROTECTION
I have no doubt that this was miraculous, from the initial telephone call which was extraordinarily accurate and precise, but it had come from an anonymous source, and what is more remarkable is the fact that when I later enquired with Belfast Regional Control, they could find no record of ever having received this phone call and they had no record of any such radio transmission to the police on the ground being despatched to my aide, it appears that no such call had ever been made. Again, I found myself asking the question of God , why had my life been spared yet again, needless to say I never did get an answer. Blessed be the name of the Lord, the hand of Almighty God continued to protect and keep me safe even though I had no idea why.

YEA, THOUGH I WALK THROUGH THE VALLEY OF THE SHADOW OF DEATH, I WILL FEAR NO EVIL.

PSALM 23 v 4 KJV

CHAPTER 5

Sandy Row Murder

To say that my first year serving in the Royal Ulster Constabulary (part-time reserve) was eventful would be a gross understatement, for what I was about to encounter was to become an incident of untold evil that would shock and stun the community and everyone involved in the follow up investigation. This was another life changing event in my relatively young life. There have been many atrocities perpetrated in Belfast during the troubles which have been both, tragic and horrific. Unfortunately this incident would become yet another statistic in a society that finds it all too easy to forget and shows no regard for the family and loved ones left behind to grieve for their tragic loss the rest of their lives.

ALPHA PAPA
By now I was fully aware of the danger involved in putting on a police uniform and the fact that a lot of people would treat you with extreme hatred and rejection because of it. However, I was not there to win any popularity prize, I was there to help in the fight against terrorism, and to help preserve life and protect property. It was on many occasions, at the expense of putting ones own life on the line to help save others. Well, I took to the task of policing like a fish to water and I enjoyed my new found role in life. I was enthusiastic and conscientious and was a willing volunteer for whatever task needed to be done. As a result I was asked if I would be willing to work a few nights each week in plain clothes, using an un-marked car, the purpose of which was to observe and report any suspicious activity around the car parks and side streets of our particular patch of south Belfast. A problem

Sandy Row Murder

existed between the hours of 7pm and 11pm when cars would be left unattended while the public attended the local cinemas. During this time there was an increase in car crime, car theft and joyriding. My job was to observe and report any suspicious activity to the control room who, would then task a uniformed patrol to assist and effect an arrest where possible. After the cinemas closed at around 11pm leaving the car parks empty, we would conduct a general patrol of the area before terminating our shift at around midnight.

On one such occasion while patrolling the side streets of Belfast's Sandy Row and Donegall Road area, we received a call on our police radio to our call sign alpha papa, informing us that a stabbing incident had occurred in Napier Street just off Sandy Row. Upon hearing this transmission we made our way to the library hill on the Donegall Road where, we took up a static mobile position in an attempt to observe any suspicious activity. Given that this location was close to the stabbing incident and had a walk way and short cut from Napier Street onto the Donegall Road. Our decision to wait and observe any movement around the periphery of the stabbing incident would prove to be a good one. We did not have long to wait, for within a matter of seconds of our

The Crescent Bar, Sandy Row, Junction with Napier Street, Belfast and scene of murder.

arrival, I observed none other than Spud running from the walk way and heading country-wards along the Donegall Road. Of course with my local knowledge I knew that Spud was likely heading in the direction of his home in the Village. The thought did cross my mind that Spud could well have been involved in the stabbing incident, but as details of the crime were still coming in, I simply completed a sighting report with Spud's movements, date and time of the sighting, a description of the clothing he was wearing at the time and the fact that he was running away from the scene of an alleged crime. The form was then submitted to the collator at Donegall Pass police station before I terminated duty.

Over the weekend I had heard various news reports on the stabbing incident and that the victim was now in the intensive care unit at the Royal Victoria Hospital in Belfast. I thought nothing more of it, until police from Donegall Pass contacted me on the Monday afternoon with a matter of urgency. I was informed that the young victim had just died and that the stabbing incident had now become a murder enquiry. I made my way to Donegall Pass police station and

Donegall Pass Police Station, Belfast.

Sandy Row Murder

spoke with the detectives in charge of the case, who were now much more interested in my sighting report of Spud and my evidence which had now become crucial to the investigation. I recorded a written statement outlining the sighting and as a result Spud was later arrested and brought into police custody on suspicion of murder. Once again I had become involved with Spud and once again my evidence had resulted in placing him in police custody. Although, this time round I had no fear of any reprisals.

Apparently what had taken place on that Saturday afternoon while Spud had been drinking in the Crescent Bar in Sandy Row, he became involved in some sort of altercation with another male person. Some-time later Spud had made his way home presumably for an evening meal. He had decided to return to the bar later that evening armed with a knife, in the hope that he might see the person he had fought with earlier. It could be argued that he had brought the knife for his own protection, but what happened later would suggest a much different reason altogether. After spending some time in the bar Spud had been at the front door of the bar looking for the return of the young man he had fought with earlier. However, he did not return back to the bar that night. The Crescent bar was a dark place with a very bad reputation and a meeting place for the local hard men. It had a reputation for drugs, underage drinking and violence. Spud stood in the shadows of the pub doorway where he spotted a younger brother of the person he had fought with earlier. Not content with letting it go and determined to get his revenge, Spud decided to chase after the young boy forcing him to run back up Napier Street towards his mother's house that he had just left a very short time earlier. When Spud caught up with him he stabbed him repeatedly then picked the young boy up and threw him through the living room window of the little terraced house, leaving him for dead. It seems that the young boy had been visiting his mother that day and was walking to the nearby bus stop to go home to his young wife and new born baby. Spud had obviously viewed this as a good opportunity to get his own back, but he chose a totally innocent person to satisfy his sick need for revenge.

Horrific as this is it fails to demonstrate just how sick, evil and twisted Spud was.

Eventually the case came to court and once again it was my evidence that helped to convict him and remove him from society, albeit, for a short time as his charge was reduced from murder to manslaughter, apparently because the prosecution failed to prove pre-meditation, so you decide, was Spud guilty of murder or manslaughter. Spud received twelve years imprisonment, of which he would serve only six years.

TO ME BELONGETH VENGEANCE, AND RECOMPENCE, THEIR FOOT SHALL SLIDE IN DUE TIME: FOR THE DAY OF THEIR CALAMITY IS AT HAND.

DEUTERONOMY 32 v 35 KJV

CHAPTER 6

The Big Decision

Although I was a part-time policeman, I was also holding down my full time job as a financial controller in a city centre office in Belfast. I had become very disillusioned with my job and the same mundane and daily routine. By now boredom had set in and I preferred the excitement and challenge that the police offered me. Ever since I can remember, all I ever wanted to do was to become a policeman. So now I was faced with having to make a big decision that would affect the rest of my life. Should I leave my job and join the full-time police force and fulfil a lifetime ambition. The decision I suppose had already been made but now I needed to take the next step. On a very wet and windy day I was walking through Belfast city centre, I was soaked to the skin with the heavy rain and I was feeling very cold and miserable. I spotted a police land-rover parked in High Street, with the back door open and its engine running. When I got closer I saw the great big lump of a policeman sprawled out across the back seat, snoring his brains out and totally oblivious to any passers-by. It was there and then I decided that I could do his job, but not ever wanting to replicate what I had just seen, as I felt that I could make a better contribution to policing than that. The big decision was made, I would join the Royal Ulster Constabulary as a full time police officer.

THE DEPOT
After passing the entrance exam, came a barrage of interviews, assessments and vetting. After what was my final interview I received a telephone call from chief inspector Basil Elliot to say that my application had been successful. I was now able to leave my office job behind and embark on a new career. Shortly afterwards I was sent to the depot in Enniskillen to

under-go my initial thirteen week training course. I arrived there on a Sunday morning and had to report to the canteen along with the other seventy one recruits. The place was packed and noisy, until someone selected a record in the duke-box. After a few seconds everyone started laughing. The record that had been selected was "suicide is painless " which, to most of us seemed quite appropriate at the time. A lot of our time was spent in the classroom studying law, but some of our time was also spent with extensive physical training, self defence, and first aid. Often we would go on six mile road runs or thirteen mile forced marches wearing great big heavy boots. Also, we went swimming in the nearby leisure centre the Lakeland Forum. The security around the police training centre was tight for fear of a terrorist attack, but there had never been an attack on any of the recruits during the troubles, and so we were confident that we would be safe and well protected.

BLOWN AWAY
After a few weeks we had become familiar with our surroundings and our daily routines when outside the training centre. However, my squad were making our way to the nearby swimming pool when a car bomb exploded en-route injuring many recruits including myself. I found myself blown off my feet and landing some distance away. After hearing the blast I went completely deaf and disorientated. I don't remember getting to my feet, but I do remember walking around in a daze before being led away. The no warning car bomb had been detonated just as we passed by the car. It was a miracle no one was killed or seriously injured. My squad, L squad, would go down in history as the only squad of new recruits to be targeted in this way. Such was the security in place at the time that the local police made two arrests within a very short period of time after the car bomb was detonated. This attack was later claimed by the provisional IRA. God had continued to protect and preserve me in the face of death and destruction.

WHO HATH DELIVERED US FROM THE POWER OF DARKNESS.

COLOSSIANS 1 v 13 KJV

Sixteen injured in IRA bomb attack

The Provisional IRA injured 16 people, five of them RUC recruits, with a no - warning car bomb explosion in the centre of Enniskillen yesterday.

The outrage came within a few hours of the announcement of the Government's concession to republican "dirty protest" prisoners in the Maze prison.

The explosion happened just as the RUC recruits were passing a car park after returning from swimming sessions at the Lakeland Forum nearby.

Eleven civilians were injured, five of them seriously. One was a 60-year-old woman who was transferred to Altnagelvin Hospital in Londonderry with a serious eye injury, while a 56-year-old woman was suffering from a heart condition. Two other civilians — a 54-year-old man and a 55-year-old woman — were also seriously injured.

The five police recruits suffered only minor injuries and last night 10 of the injured were still in hospital.

The Provisional IRA admitted the bombing.

The mass murder bid has brought a wave of bitter revulsion, coming as it did on the day the Government "caved in" to the republican prisoners in the H-Blocks.

The recruits were returning from their customary afternoon swimming session and life-saving training at the Forum. They usually run the three-quarter-mile from the pool to the training centre.

☐ Above — A young policeman, one of the victims of Provisional IRA terror on the day the Government bowed to republican demands on the H - Block issue.
☐ Right — The car in which the bomb had been planted.

Their normal route is along a path and through a narrow gap at the end of a row of shops at one side of Paget Square. The car containing the bomb had been left at one side of the gap, between a hedge and the side wall of one of the shops.

There were other cars in the park in front of the row of shops. It was market day in Enniskillen and the area was crowded.

Continued in Page 2, col. nine

*Newspaper Article re:
Attack on RUC Training Centre.*

CHAPTER 7

Shantallow - Londonderry

Before passing out of the training centre terrorist activity was intensifying and the police found themselves stretched to breaking point. The authorities could not get recruits trained quick enough and out on to the streets. So before we had passed out of the training centre our squad of new recruits was sent to Portadown, in order to back up the regular police who were on public order duties. For a new police officer there was nowhere in the province that could be considered a safe place to be stationed, but we were offered a choice of stations at an interview prior to leaving the training centre, or so I thought. The interview was with the commandant of the training centre along with other senior ranking officers. During which time I was asked where I would like to serve. I was confident that I would never be given a Belfast posting as I was a native of Belfast, so I really had no preference. I was absolutely sure that the one place I did not want to serve in was Londonderry, and I made that quite clear at my interview. I had only ever visited Londonderry once, for a few hours and I took an instant dislike to it. So I said that I would be happy to serve anywhere else in Northern Ireland except Londonderry. However a few days later I was officially informed that I was being sent to N-Division, yes it was Londonderry. Later I got news that my first station was to be Shantallow RUC station which was based inside Fort George, British Army Camp and was regarded as extremely high risk. Londonderry was of course, a provisional IRA stronghold and I knew just how volatile it could be. Disappointment comes nowhere close to describing how I felt upon hearing

40

Shantallow - Londonderry

such news, but there it was, nothing could be done to change things now I would have to grin and bear it.

I felt that I had been thrown into the lion's den, for I was to encounter a savage and brutal onslaught of hatred and violence upon my arrival which at that time was beyond my comprehension. That was before I was to see any active service because in my attempt to get to Fort George I had to run a gauntlet of rioting, dodging bottles and stones along Strand Road. They must have known that I was coming that day so perhaps they wanted to welcome me in the only way they knew how.

THEY CAST HIM INTO THE DEN OF LIONS

DANIEL 6 v 24 KJV

Shantallow, IRA stronghold, Londonderry.

Born Again - The Man They Couldn't Kill

British Army under attack during IRA hunger strike at Trench Road, Gobnascale, Londonderry.

Masked Youths armed with Petrol Bombs rioting in Londonderry during IRA hunger strike.

CHAPTER 8

Drunken Nights

Such was the pressures of having to cope with the constant onslaught of relentless violence a pre-occupation of most serving police officers during the troubles was alcohol. Not that anyone needed a reason to drink, but, the heavy consumption of alcohol was always blamed on the pressure of the troubles. While there can be no doubt that the things we had to deal with were at times enough to break the hardest of men's resolve, given the trail of death and destruction which had now become a way of life, there were some who found it imposable to cope and many became alcoholics or some ended up committing suicide, such was the pressure. As a young Christian and with no other Christian colleagues I had to bear the brunt of mockery and scorn from my fellow colleagues. Like so many before me I was stationed on what could be called the front line of the troubles and some of my experiences had a diverse effect on my own life at that time and, in the years that followed.

I was to deviate from my walk with the Lord to sample the way of the world and partake of the demon drink. It was often said that the things we experienced was enough to drive anyone to drink and I was no exception. Over and above the daily routine of policing and the hard man persona that most of us had adopted to help us cope, all of a sudden here I was having to attend the scene of many fatal road traffic accidents, suicides and sudden deaths, not to mention shootings and bombings. I had to attend many post mortem examinations as part of my duty was to take notes for the pathologist as it was necessary for the investigating officer to record the preliminary cause of death. Post mortems were never really a problem for me, once you had become aware of the procedures, and you had experienced the sounds and smells associated with the examinations. However, not all victims were old or middle aged, and it all became too much for me when I investigated my first cot death. When I saw a baby on the slab and an autopsy being performed on one so young that I was unable and unwilling to be present and on such occasions, I would always ask the pathologist if I could be excused. It is still painful for me today as I recall such tragic memories.

During my service I had more than my share of attending horrific scene's, and many bizarre and disturbing incidents. I have had to dig through the rubble of bombed out buildings in an effort to locate and rescue dead bodies and survivors, mostly, with horrific injuries and missing limbs. Also on occasions I had to search the countryside picking up body parts of fellow human beings and placing their body parts into brown paper bags which were then handed to their family members to be placed in a coffin for a Christian burial. I have seen so many family's torn apart by grief and to witness the aftermath of lives destroyed forever was just heartbreaking.

So I suffered as did many police officers to the extent that my walk with God had grown cold. There was no Christian fellowship and I was never at home long enough to go to church, and so I fell into a backslidden state and before long I had hit the drink. The army officers mess provided us all with ridiculously cheap drink, and when drinking my conscience would always remind me that, what I was about to do was wrong, but no matter how reluctant I was to take that first drink, inevitably it was taken, followed by another and another, until I was so drunk I needed help to get back to my room. There I would fall asleep totally oblivious to anything or anyone. This pattern continued, and much to my shame it would be repeated for several years to come. There were also times when I would drink and drive and on many occasions I would be so drunk when driving many miles back to my home I was unable remember how I got there or if I had had an accident, killing or injuring someone, because of the state I was in. So many mornings I have

Drunken Nights

woken up in the horrors of drink and severely hung over and remembering nothing from the night before. I would run outside to check for sign's of damage to my car. Always, I would find my car parked perfectly in its appropriate space and in perfect condition. I was shocked and amazed at how this could be possible. The only explanation possible and the only explanation I believe there can be, is that of divine intervention, when I was blind drunk and oblivious to all things around me, and, I was totally incapable of driving my car that God sent his angels to drive me home safely, and to park my car. There is no other explanation.

You may well have heard that people who smoked cigarettes and have been able to give them up, now hate smoking with a vengeance, well, since alcohol had a grip on my life and I have seen first-hand the trail of devastation it causes, and how Satan can and will use alcohol to destroy people's lives, I also hate alcohol with a passion. In my experience, Satan uses alcohol to destroy the lives of so many good people to break up and destroy marriages. Those who drink are, in my opinion bad company for Christians. Listen to what the scripture says.

WINE IS A MOCKER, STRONG DRINK IS RAGING: AND WHOSOEVER IS DECEIVED THEREBY IS NOT WISE.

PROVERBS 20 v 1

CHAPTER 9

Divine Protection

I had arrived in Londonderry at the beginning of 1981, just at the start of the IRA hunger strike. At this time the British government were under pressure to meet the demands of the hunger strikers for political status. On the 1st of March 1981 the first prisoner refused food, as the dirty protest by republican prisoners in the Maze and Armagh prisons was called off in order to focus sole attention on the hunger strike. However, the British government refused to give in to their demands as the National H – Block committee sponsored demonstrations throughout Ireland. There was support from around the world and also from the Roman Catholic Church in Ireland led by the then primate of all Ireland Tomas O'Fiaich. As the outpouring of support continued to grow, the tension also continued to grow and, inevitably the protests and marches turned to violence and great civil unrest. Rioting on a wide scale across the province escalated with an increase in hijackings, shootings and bomb attacks on a daily basis. The security forces were now at full stretch and working around the clock in a futile effort to keep the peace.

During a hunger strike protest march on Strand Road, Londonderry, I found myself on the front line of a police cordon in an attempt to prevent the protesters entering the city centre, when I was pulled from the police line into a raging mob and subjected to an animal like attack. I was thrown to the ground as the mob of men, women and children started kicking and punching me, with some using sticks and umbrellas to beat me. I had never seen such hatred in all my life. It seemed like time had stood still before I was rescued by my colleagues from the Divisional Mobile Support Unit, (DMSU) who had to baton charge the protesters to effect

Divine Protection

my rescue. Needless to say by that stage I had sustained injuries, fortunately they were of a minor nature and I was able to rejoin my colleagues. This incident I regarded as my official welcome to the City of Londonderry which left a lasting impression on my life and something I will never forget.

Bogside, Londonderry.

As the hunger strike gathered momentum and the unrest continued to escalate the British Prime Minister, Margaret Thatcher refused to negotiate with the hunger strikers and so as a result the first hunger striker died on 5 May 1981. The violence that followed was on a scale never seen before, resulting in the guns being brought onto the streets in an effort to kill any members of the security forces they could. To make matters worse another hunger striker died on 12 May 1981 adding more fuel to a fire which was already burning out of control and with such ferocity. Now the murderous intent from the provisional IRA would see almost every police patrol subject to both bomb and gun attack anytime they entered a republican area. We could now only travel in heavily armoured land-rovers which would also be attacked by petrol bombs, paint bombs and a recent introduction of acid bombs was introduced which would be thrown at policemen while on foot. Well, I felt some degree of safety given that all our police vehicles were armour plated and offered some degree of protection. Then the IRA started using armour piercing rounds and RPG 7 rocket launchers, which were capable of cutting through our land-rovers like a knife through butter. So much for feeling safe, as we were now sitting ducks ready to be picked off at will. We never knew when such an attack would take place.

THERE SHALL NO EVIL BEFALL THEE.

PSALM 91 V 10

CHAPTER 10

Angels Watching Over Me

On one occasion in May 1981 I was part of a patrol operating in six land-rovers in the Shantallow area of Londonderry. Crowds of rioting youths had gathered on the Racecourse Road and had started attacking local business premises. The street lighting had been destroyed and the area was in complete darkness. They were now hijacking cars and buses and setting them on fire. Our briefing had been simply to protect property and quell the rioting. We came under sustained attack from petrol bombs over a period of about three hours and despite being backed up by British Army snatch squads, we could not contain the rioting. We then received a radio transmission requesting us to withdraw to a nearby car park at Stewart's supermarket on the Racecourse Road in order to take a break and to re-group before going back into the rioting. As all six land-rovers pulled into the car park and personnel had started to de-bus from their vehicles a gunman opened fire and, as the shots rang out and everyone was franticly running to take cover I happened to be the last person in the last vehicle attempting to clear the land-rover and run to safety. Just as I got to the rear door of the vehicle I became aware that the gunman was in fact shooting at my vehicle. I heard the sound of bullets striking all around me, so I froze not knowing if I should make a run for it or get back inside the land-rover. I had no decision to make as a stray round narrowly missed me and was now ricocheting around the inside of my vehicle. Then I heard an explosion as I was flung from the vehicle, landing several feet away, face down in the car park. I was aware of bullets landing around my head and the smell of cordite as I felt bits of grit hitting my head and lodging in my hair. Then an unbelievable sense of peace came over

49

me and a verse of scripture came in to my mind, "FOR HE SHALL GIVE HIS ANGELS CHARGE OVER THEE, TO KEEP THEE IN ALL THY WAYS". (Psalm 91 v 11). When the shooting had stopped I discovered that the stray round had lodged in the fire extinguisher which had then exploded, the force of which blew me out of the land-rover and on to the ground. After we examined the scene of the shooting, I saw the exact place were my head had been and discovered that the strike marks from the bullets had formed a perfect circle around my head, and yet not one single hair on my head had been harmed. There is no doubt in my mind that I had experienced a miracle from God. I am also convinced that I had only survived because God did actually send his angels to protect and watch over me. This was a life changing experience which drew me closer to God and, my walk with Him became far more meaningful and real.

Car Park and high ground where the shooting took place.

Angels Watching Over Me

THE FOLLOW UP
After every major incident the police will always conduct a follow up operation, and in this case they were supported by the British Army. It appeared that the gunman had opened fire from the high ground in a housing estate overlooking the car park. At that location police recovered a high powered snipers rifle and a number of spent bullet cases. It was extraordinary for an IRA gunman to leave such a highly prized weapon behind for the security forces to recover, which indicated that the gunman had left the scene in a hurry immediately after the attack.

FOR HE SHALL GIVE HIS ANGELS CHARGE OVER THEE, TO KEEP THEE IN ALL THY WAYS.

THEY SHALL BEAR THEE UP IN THEIR HANDS, LEST THOU DASH THY FOOT AGAINST A STONE.

PSALMS 91 v 11-12

Armoured RUC Landrover showing paint and petrol bomb damage, similar to the one in which I survived gun attack.

CHAPTER 11

The Only Man I Couldn't Kill

A few years later I was involved in a secret operation acting as part of a team providing backup to the RUC special branch and Army intelligence officers. The operation was the removal of a well known terrorist suspect and member of the provisional IRA from an address in the Shantallow area of Londonderry. Because of the highly classified and secret nature of this operation we had been briefed only at the last minute, so as to avoid compromising the incident. All agencies involved moved swiftly while maintaining radio silence and using only code words if required. The operation was a complete success with the subject being placed in protective custody. We had been instructed to maintain silence regarding the operation and were told to talk to no one about what had just taken place. We had no information to impart anyway but, this operation was unusually secretive and seemed to involve other members of the security services I believed to be MI5.

The next day I was approached by a special branch officer, who told me to go to the interview room where someone wanted to meet me. Thinking the person in the interview room was perhaps a colleague from another police station who had enquired if I was on duty that day and wanted to speak with me. I had no hesitation in entering the interview room. As I recognised the special branch officer in the room I asked him if he wanted to see me. He pointed to the other person in the room and said, he wants to meet you. I also recognised the other person as a well known terrorist suspect, whose mug shot decorated the walls of every police

The Only Man I Couldn't Kill

station in Londonderry. Needless to say, I was shocked and speechless, that this person wanted to meet me. What on earth did he want with me. He walked towards me smiling and then he shook my hand. I was still in disbelief. Then he asked me if I remembered being shot at in the car park of Stewart's supermarket in Shantallow a few years ago. Stilled shocked by his question I replied " yes, I will never forget it, why " He looked me in the eye and said in a quiet voice, " I am the gunman who shot at you that night." I was stunned, however he went on to explain that he was a trained marksman, and an experienced sniper who had always hit his target, and never missed anything he aimed at. He then said, the high powered snipers rifle he had used in the attack had already been zeroed in, for he did it himself earlier that day. As my heart started to race, he told me, " I just wanted to shake the hand of *the only man I couldn't kill.*" So, despite my shock I could only manage a smile, but knowing full well that it had been God alone who had protected me, and that was the real reason why he could not kill me. This had a profound effect on his life he said, because he panicked for the first time in his life and in his state of disbelief he just ran away leaving his rifle behind, something he would never have done. Now he was facing extreme investigation and discipline from the IRA for leaving such a prized weapon behind to be recovered by the police. Again I listened speechless as he told me that his failure to shoot me, had caused him to question why he was trying to kill anyone. His conscience had troubled him greatly and after much deliberation and soul searching he made the decision to contact the RUC Special Branch and become an informer. While he continued on active service for the IRA, the information he provided to the security forces went on to save many lives and frustrate future IRA operations for quite some time. Time had now run out for him, and his double life was catching up on him. It had become much too dangerous as the Provo's had now suspected him of being an informer. The time had come to bring him in, to give him a new identity and relocate him somewhere safe to start a new life in another country.

"GOD WORKS IN MYSTERIOUS WAYS HIS WONDERS TO PERFORM"

CHAPTER 12

Covert Operations

In 1983 the authorities in N-Division had been faced with a growing problem in Strabane, County Tyrone. Republican activity had intensified and the number of terrorist attacks had increased to the extent that things were now getting out of control. The local police had come under severe pressure and were now stretched to breaking point. Local police were coming under attack every time they left the station on foot patrol, and it was recognised that something had to be done to restore some sort of control.

The plan was to form a specialised anti terrorist response unit operating in small cells, in a covert capacity by providing support to the local police and be able to operate in an undercover surveillance role. Due to the nature of the work applications were requested on a volunteer only basis as we would be working in conjunction with RUC special branch and elite British Army regiments. I became a member of this unit known as N2 and was based at the camels hump army camp within a few yards of the border between Lifford, County Donegal and Strabane.

Our movements were mostly restricted to the hours of darkness as we operated in ghost cars (unmarked police vehicles) capable of unusually high speeds. On occasions we would be air lifted by army helicopter and dropped off several miles from our OP (observation point). There we would dig in and spend extended periods of time, before being extracted.

The nature of these operations were classified as secret, and as a result I don't want to talk any further about this three year period of my service or to be in breach of the official secrets act. Suffice to say that the hand of God was ever present on my life during this difficult and most dangerous time.

TO SPY OUT THE LAND, AND TO SEARCH IT:

JUDGES CH.18 V2. KJV

CHAPTER 13

Suffer Little Children

Time moved on but, the situation across the province remained the same with no let up in the troubles. After having made several requests for a transfer to a Belfast station turned down, I eventually received some good news. I was to be transferred to E-Division in Belfast. Soon I was to learn that my new station was in fact Castlereagh, the notorious Castlereagh holding centre, where most of the terrorist suspects were taken for interview when arrested under the Emergency Provisions Act.

After a short time there, I was finding it difficult to make the adjustment from anti-terrorism type duties to the more normal and mundane policing that I had never experienced before. I found that my new colleagues were a different breed than what I had been used to, there was not the same comradeship that I had experienced while in border stations. Instead of them covering your back, they were more likely to stab you in the back, for reasons only they would know. I just kept my head down and continued to work to the best of my ability. I was never really happy there and it did take quite some time for me to adopt to non confrontational police work.

BACK HOME TO THE VILLAGE
This transfer meant that for many years I had been away from Belfast and so I now found myself back living at home with my parents albeit, on a temporary basis until I could find a place of my own. Given what had happened to me in the past, living at home was not really a good idea. It would not take long for my suspicions to be realised. I had been living at home for about two weeks and had been travelling

Born Again - The Man They Couldn't Kill

back and forward to work experiencing no real problems. I was always vigilant and would always check underneath my car for under car booby trap devices which had been a fairly successful way of killing members of the security forces. It was now a way of life for people and I also knew that my neighbours would also be looking out for anything they thought was suspicious and that they would alert me if necessary.

I had finished my early shift one day and I had been home for quite some time, when I heard a flurry of activity and a loud knock at the front door. "My goodness, who on earth is that at the door." I got to the door first only to be pushed inside by a police sergeant and told to get a bag packed as quickly as possible. I had no time to ask him why, as he had made it clear that they needed to get me out of the house now. By this stage I noticed that our street had been cordoned off with several Police Land Rovers, but I still did not know why. An explanation was given to my parents when I returned into the room. My mother was in a terrible state and was being consoled by a police woman. Without explanation I was rushed to one of the Land-Rovers which was parked outside my house, and I was flanked by several heavily armed members of the D.M.S.U. As I was taken away I observed crowds of onlookers who were as bewildered as I was. I was then transported to secure accommodation at Castlereagh RUC Station to be debriefed by special branch. They told me that they had received reliable information to suggest that I was going to be shot that very night. I was then assigned a small room which would be my home for the foreseeable future. I was concerned now for my parents personal safety if such an attack was to be carried out. I was informed that my parents were fully aware of the situation and that police protection was provided for them.

The next day I was interviewed by special branch officers who informed me they had received a telephone call in which the caller named me personally and said that I was going to be shot that night. Acting on this information they set up a meeting with the caller as a matter of urgency in order to obtain more detailed information. I was then given

Suffer Little Children

a name of a person and asked if I knew him. I replied "yes" then they asked me how I knew this person and I said that I had been his Sunday school teacher some twenty years ago when he was just a wee boy. They looked at each other and confirmed that our accounts were the same. They then told me this person was now a loyalist gunman who had been given orders to shoot me along with another accomplice. The story goes that a plan had been hatched to lure me out of the house. They would know that I was at home when they saw my car parked outside the house. The plan then was to throw a petrol bomb through the downstairs window and when I would exit the house through the front door two gunmen would step forward and shoot me. When the gunman was asked why he wanted to save my life he said "Jim was my Sunday school teacher and he's a really good person and I don't want to shoot him." God's hand of

Castlereagh RUC Station where I was placed in secure accommodation.

divine protection had saved my life once again. This is the young man I spoke about earlier, the one who disrupted my Sunday school class, trying my patience all those years ago. He went on to work for the RUC Special Branch, helping to save lives that otherwise may have been lost.

I thank God that he allowed me into this young man's life as I sought to teach him about Jesus at Sunday school in Kilburn Street, Belfast City Mission hall. Remember seed sown is not seed wasted. So a word to everyone involved in church work with young people please persevere with all the kids you work with, especially those who are more troublesome, and challenging, you never know the results of seed sown. In my case it just saved my life.

SUFFER LITTLE CHILDREN TO COME UNTO ME, AND FORBID THEM NOT: FOR SUCH IS THE KINGDOM OF GOD.

MARK 10 v 14 KJV

CHAPTER 14

Medical Discharge

As a police officer I had seen service in Londonderry, Strabane, Belfast, Newcastle and Ballykinler Army Camp. Most of my service had been spent in border stations. I served in numerous different departments of the RUC including CID and the major incident room at Strandtown operating the Home Office Large Major Enquiry System, (H.O.L.M.E.S). You are well aware by now that I have experienced many horrific scenes and atrocities, some of which I have been able to relate to you, while others I am unable and unwilling to relate at this time.

One point I would like to make is that despite all my years of dedicated and faithful service I am left in no doubt, that working for the government as a proud member of the RUC, I am just a number like everyone else who has put their life on the line, for what? Since the demise of the RUC the authorities have turned on their own, many former colleagues have been hunted down and dragged through the courts as scapegoats for their sacrifice and faithful obedience in carrying out orders for the greater good of our country and its citizens. I view this as an act of appeasement to the real enemies of our beloved country. We can trust no one, but almighty God who never changes or who never lets us down, for he is the same yesterday, today and forever, praise His name.

I was medically discharged from the RUC for injuries I sustained in a shooting incident. I know with certainty that God brought me through these years of conflict and delivered me to the place where I would now open a new chapter in my life and, I was convinced that I may not see His hand at work in my life to the same extent now I was retired. I was set to live a dull and hopefully uneventful life from now on. How wrong I was, for as one chapter of my life ended, another one begun. So, the remaining chapters of this book will demonstrate the hand of God continuing to work in my life in a powerful and miraculous way.

BUT UNTO YOU THAT FEAR MY NAME SHALL THE SON OF RIGHTEOUSNESS ARISE WITH HEALING IN HIS WINGS.

MALACHI 4 v 2

The Royal Ulster Constabulary
MEMORIAL

A total of 300 RUC officers have been murdered during the Troubles. The IRA has killed 277, the INLA and IPLO 12 and loyalist terrorists eight. Three were murdered by unknown groups. In addition, four officers were killed by the security forces by mistake and over 9,000 injured during the course of their duties.

Terrorist groups have bombed, shot and beaten RUC officers to death, sometimes killing relatives and other civilians in the process. Levels of stress-related illness have been higher than in any other police force: almost 70 officers have commmitted suicide, many of them with RUC-issued weapons.

RUC Badge

George Cross Medal

CHAPTER 15

Stanley Close

In 1988 I married Jennifer, and in addition to getting a wife I also got a father in law, a mother in law and a lot of brothers and sisters in law. However, my father in law was Stanley Close, who was a good father in law to me and a good man to all who knew him. I found him to be a respectful, decent and quiet man who just lived for his family and grandchildren. He was not a religious man but he did respect that Jennifer and I were Christians. Over the years that followed we did on one occasion give him a bible as a birthday present. We cannot be sure if he ever read the bible but, we do know that he treasured it. Stanley was not the type of man you could ever speak to about God or his need of salvation although, that's not to say that he never thought about these things in private. We understand that he had wondered about what would happen to him when he died, but to the best of our knowledge he did nothing to satisfy his curiosity. So, every day in life Jennifer and I committed Stanley and other family members to prayer in the hope that God would save their souls.

Stanley had been diagnosed with cancer around 1993 and for many years he suffered the ravages of the disease in dignified silence. Over the years the illness took its toll resulting in him having to be hospitalised on numerous occasions. After having surgery to remove a kidney he rallied for a short time before being told that he would need to have his other kidney removed. This resulted in him needing dialysis every day. So he had a decision to make, if he lost his other kidney it would extend his life by approximately twelve months. If he refused, the doctors gave him about six months to live.

Despite the doctor's advice, Stanley decided that surgery was not an option. I imagine that because he had suffered so much over so many years he had now become weary and enough was enough. The doctors had written him off on so many occasions before when he was at death's door and had given him no hope, but Stanley always fought back and made miraculous recoveries which would defy his doctors.

Everyone knew that Stanley's time on this earth was drawing to an end so, rather than ram the bible down his throat, which we know would have been a big mistake, Jennifer and I asked God for a miracle and hoped that God would provide an opportunity before it was too late. We had been praying faithfully for Stanley for the past seventeen years and we trusted God to intervene and save his soul.

TIME IS RUNNING OUT
When Stanley was taken into hospital at the end of November 2003 he quickly slipped into a state of unconsciousness and for days he was unable to communicate with the family as they kept a vigil at his bedside. Nothing short of a miracle could save him now. Jennifer and I were not about to give up hope as we continued to pray for Stanley. We had great faith, but we had no idea how God would intervene as time was running out.

THE MIRACLE
On Sunday 7 December 2003 I had a very restless night, I lay tossing and turning in bed and calling out to God for a miracle. Despite my anxiety and frustration, once again a peace fell over me and I heard God speaking to me and gently telling me to go to the hospital the next day and speak to Stanley, and he would do the rest. I pondered these words and questioned if it was my imagination, maybe I was so frantic that I had hoped it was God who had spoken, but could it just be me hoping beyond all hope for some sort of miracle. I was demented, but this was a very clear and specific command, so I decided to go to the Belfast City Hospital the next morning and see Stanley, believing that God would do the rest.

The next morning I had a 6.00am start with my work and so I made my way to Newry in the hope that I could get away early enough to get to the hospital. I had an uncomfortable journey and was unable to get Stanley out of my mind. I had felt that visiting the hospital at 6.00am was far too early, but I had no idea what time I should go there at. I had arrived outside my destination and I decided to pray. I had only uttered a few words before I felt the Lord telling me to go to the hospital now. I immediately turned my car around and headed for Belfast. I ran into traffic jam after traffic jam, then, extensive road works followed by a pile up on the M1 motorway. I could sense a dark cloud following me as I felt that Satan was doing everything in his power to stop me getting to the hospital. I prayed and I prayed all the way to the Belfast City Hospital, and I knew that my next problem would be getting a car parking space at that time of the morning, so I prayed for a car parking space. On my arrival I immediately found a car parking space close to the front of the hospital, and I thanked God. As I was walking through the corridors I kept praying that I would be in time. I got to the lift and found the lift door already opened as if it was being held open by angels, with no one inside. When I got to the hospital ward I spoke to an oriental doctor and asked him if I could see Stanley Close. He told me I could but, he is in a coma and will not be able to communicate with you. My heart was pounding as I gingerly pulled back the screen from around his bed. When I saw him I thought that he was already dead as all I saw was a skeleton of a man with leads and machines keeping him alive. In my despair I stepped forward and I rubbed his left arm. Immediately Stanley sat up in bed and spoke. He actually frightened me as this was the last thing I expected. He said "Ah Jim it's good to see you." I can't even remember my reply I was that shocked. His face lit up and he was smiling as I said these words, "Stanley, I have known you for 17 years now and in all that time I have never asked you for anything." I know, he said. "Now, I want to ask you to do something for me, just listen to me for the next few minutes." He agreed, and I got straight to the point. In the few minutes that followed I was able to lead Stanley to the Lord as he prayed the sinner's prayer with me. He became radiant, but I could see his frailty and so I shook his hand and said my goodbyes.

I was overcome with emotion, mixed with relief and an overwhelming sense of God's awesome power and endless mercy. Moments later I was back in the lift heading for the exit. However, as I was going down in one lift, Stanley's son and brother were going up in the other lift to the ward to see Stanley. I am told that when they got to Stanley's bed he had slipped back into a coma. I had left Stanley at 10am that morning and Stanley left us at 10pm that night to go to be with the Lord.

I had the great privilege of saying a few words at Stanley's graveside, and while some family members found this miracle hard to believe for a variety of reasons, not least that they had never experienced a miracle before, it gave me a wonderful opportunity to witness to them. They were left in no doubt that they to, needed the Lord Jesus Christ as their saviour to obtain everlasting life, but, so that they could be reunited with Stanley again in eternity.

THE FINAL WORD READ AT STANLEY'S FUNERAL

Born: 23rd August 1930. Born Again: 8th December 2003

John 14 vv 1-3
(1) Let not your heart be troubled, ye believe in God, believe also in me.
(2) In my Father's house are many mansions: if it were not so I would have told you. I go to prepare a place for you.
(3) And if I go to prepare a place for you, I will come again, and receive you unto myself, that where I am, there you may be also.

Early on Monday morning I had the privilege of speaking to Stanley for a short time. He was fully aware of who I was and what I was saying. He wanted me to pray with him and, during that prayer, he found faith in God. I was able to tell him that he had absolutely nothing to fear now. I told him that this was the greatest gift he had ever given to his family because, now, we would be able to see him again in Heaven. He smiled and said, "*I know*"; his face lit up with joy. I told him that we all loved him and that we would see him again in Heaven. He grabbed my hand, smiled and gave me the thumbs up. I left him at a quarter past ten in the morning, he left us at a quarter past ten in the evening on Monday 8th December, 2003 to be with God in Heaven. At peace at last.

Stanley Close

CHAPTER 16

My Son James

On 30 June 2007, we were to receive news that would change our lives again. My seventeen year old son James was involved in a serious road traffic accident while a front seat passenger in a car. I was downstairs when a knock came to my front door. From the loud, decisive knock I knew instinctively there was bad news coming. My heart sank and started beating faster as I made my way to the front door. On my approach to the door I could see two uniformed police officers; I could hardly get a breath as I saw their bright luminous coats and sombre faces, I had a terrible sinking feeling which made me feel physically sick. I opened the door, by now breathless and with an indescribable fear as I looked at the police woman's face which left me in no doubt that this would be the worst news imaginable.

"Are you Mr. Stewart" she asked. "Do you have a son named James"? "I'm afraid he has been involved in an accident". She was compassionate and sorrowful and without speaking another word, I sensed that James must be dead. I was numb as my wife joined me at the door, she was screaming and crying and in the seconds that followed we were informed that in fact James was still alive but we needed to get to the hospital as a matter of extreme urgency. We drove straight to the Royal Victoria Hospital. On my way there I made one telephone call to activate our church prayer chain.

We arrived at the hospital as if in no time at all where I abandoned our car and ran into the Accident and Emergency Department. We were taken to a private room, which again indicated to me that we should expect the worst. Then eventually, the consultant from accident and emergency came and spoke to us telling us that James was still alive, BUT, he stated that things were not looking good and that his injuries had left him in a critical condition and he may not survive. He told us to prepare for the worst. We were told that James had suffered horrendous injuries as we pleaded with him not to let him die. He assured us that he would do all he could to keep him alive, but there were no guarantees.

I was then called away to another room with my wife where a nurse handed me a large clear plastic bag containing our son's personal effects. The bottom of the bag was partially filled with his blood; this was unexpected as we were not prepared for such an horrific sight as his clothes, or what remained of them along with some items of jewellery which were submerged in blood. This was far too much for his mother to bear and she collapsed, screaming and crying. To see his clothes that had been cut from his body sent a chill down my spine.

Several long hours had passed before we were told that James was being transferred to the Intensive Care Unit and that we should make our way there. It was at this stage we were told that James had sustained a number of broken bones with severe head injuries and quite extensive damage to his brain. At around 5.00pm we were allowed in to see James, but we were not prepared for what we were about to see. James was in a side ward attached to innumerable machines with tubes everywhere. He was totally paralysed, and a life support machine now breathing for him. He was not recognisable as our son. This was the most horrific sight we had ever seen.

HORRENDOUS INJURIES
It was only then that we discovered James had been the front seat passenger in a vehicle driven by an acquaintance who had been speeding along a country road when the car left the road and rolled across a field. Fortunately, James was wearing a seatbelt at the time. So Saturday 30 June 2007 as our son lay in Intensive Care fighting for his life the full extent of his injuries were about to be revealed:

Car in which James was the front seat passenger.

James had died three times at the scene of the accident and was resuscitated by paramedics. He had a severe brain injury to four different parts of his brain, as well as a brain stem injury and a brain haemorrhage, with blood escaping from the only place available, his right eye. He had a broken neck and had a broken back in two places, a broken jaw, smashed cheekbone, broken upper palate and a broken nose. He had severed an artery in his cheek which caused him to almost bleed to death at the scene, James had a severe wound to the back of his head with numerous other injuries to his body and upper body. He had also suffered collapsed lungs, a torn oesophagus and extensive facial swelling and bruising.

When confronted with this information we knew that his survival had been a miracle. His medical notes read as follows:

Saturations 92%
Heart rate 120 per minute
BP 180/100

Glasgow Coma Score 3/15
Pupils fixed and dilated.

These vital signs reflect the extent of his condition and although unknown to us at the time, we were to discover later on just had serious things had been.

FEAR NOT; FOR I AM WITH THEE; BE NOT DISMAYED; FOR I AM THY GOD; I WILL STRENGTHEN THEE; I WILL KEEP THEE; YEA, I WILL UPHOLD THEE WITH THE RIGHT HAND OF MY RIGHTEOUSNESS.

ISAIAH 41 v 10

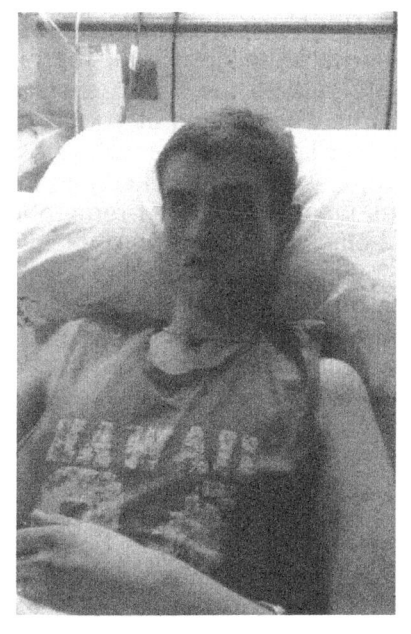

James recovering in R.A.B.I.U. Musgrave Park Hospital, Belfast.

CHAPTER 17

Stranger: Angel or Messenger

We now had lost count of the number of visits we had made each day to the I.C.U. and sometimes we would have to leave James during the various ward rounds to allow the doctors and nurses to work with him. However on Monday 2 July 2007 we were returning to our room at around lunch time from the I.C.U. after leaving James. We had to walk through the waiting area to get to our room. When inside the room, my wife said to me, "Did you see the man in the waiting room; he was looking at you as if you had two heads." As it happens I did see a man who stood out from all the rest of the people who were packed into the room at the time. For reasons unknown to me I remembered seeing a man dressed in a black suit, white shirt, black tie and black coloured shoes. My immediate thought was that this person may have been someone who had called to see me and enquire about James, although I had no idea who this could be. For fear of appearing rude, I walked outside to see who this stranger could be, but within a few seconds and despite my search of the waiting room and hospital corridors, he had vanished.

Two days later, on Wednesday 4th July 2007, Jennifer and I had spent most of the morning at James' bedside. We had watched as his condition deteriorated and the monitors indicated that things were not good, which became more and more obvious given the flurry of activity from the nursing staff, we decided to let them work with him and we should go back to our little room and pray through this situation and ask God to intervene, until his condition improved. We were so anxious to get back to prayer that we almost ran back to our room.

Stranger: Angel or Messenger

We got as far as the door of the waiting room, and before I could step inside I saw a hand go up as if to stop me, and it did, there was the same man from two days earlier, sitting in the same seat and wearing exactly the same clothes. This time he had what appeared to be a Bible in his hand. I was stopped dead in my tracks when he spoke. "Are you Jim?" I said yes. "Are you Jim Stewart," again I answered yes. Jennifer and I walked towards him and I got really close to him and said, "I'm sorry but I don't know you," to which he said, "No, you wouldn't know me." The stranger then went on to explain he was here visiting someone in the Intensive Care Unit, explaining that I would know the person he was here to see. Before we could respond he had stood to his feet and started shaking our hands. As Jennifer was explaining that we had a son in Intensive Care, he said, "Can we go into your room as I would like to pray for you." We closed the door and sat down. As the stranger started to pray, immediately the peace of God fell upon us from Heaven, and filled the little room. All our anxiety, all our worries and all our stress just faded away and were gone in an instant. The peace and contentment, the like of which we had never experienced before, just filled our souls. His prayer was short, no more than two minutes, but it was the most powerful and productive prayer we had ever heard. We cannot remember with any accuracy the prayer, but we were transported from our hellish reality, into the presence and tranquillity of Almighty God. When the prayer ended we enjoyed a brief moment of silence to bask and be refreshed in God's glory.

Then the stranger gestured to me as though he was strumming a guitar. I was surprised and asked him what he was doing. "Remember," he said, "You used to sing in a gospel group." My wife and I laughed as she told the stranger that I had told this story to our kids on numerous occasions, but they were never sure it was true. "Oh yes," he said, "You did some great work for the Lord back then." I told him that was some forty years ago and even I could not remember too much about it. Then he referred to my Sunday school teacher, stating that she is still teaching Sunday School today, just over fifty years now. The stranger went on to say, sure she was the one who led you to the Lord when you were seven years old in the front seat of Kilburn Street, Belfast City Mission hall after the children's meeting on the Monday night.

At this point I was flabbergasted, because here was a man who knew my whole life story from my childhood and I didn't have a clue who he was. Then I asked him who he was and where he came from, or did we go to school together or grow up together. He said, "You wouldn't know me, I am not from here," despite his local accent. He then stood up and reached Jennifer a gospel tract and he told us he had to go now, back into intensive care. He shook our hands and walked out of the room, Jennifer and I looked at each other as we followed him out into the waiting room. He turned left out the door and into the corridor with us following behind him. The stranger turned left through the set of double doors into the hallway leading into the Intensive Care Unit. Then, before our eyes he just disappeared, gone without trace, nowhere to be seen. We just looked at each other unable to take in what had happened. As there was nowhere for him to go, we decided to search for him as the only door in front of him was the I.C.U. I decided to start there. Now as everyone knows you don't just walk into I.C.U. as the doors are always locked and an intercom system is used to request entry before admission can be granted, the staff must conduct a check before allowing anyone in. This procedure usually takes about two minutes. So when I eventually got into I.C.U. I enquired of the staff if anyone had come into the unit in the past few minutes. I was told that Jennifer and I were the last persons to go in and come out in the past thirty minutes.

The mystery did not end there, for when Jennifer opened up the little Gospel tract that the stranger had left, she read these words, "But the very hairs on your head are numbered, Matthew 10 v 30," the very same verse that we prayed for James every single day since he was admitted to hospital. We have no explanation as to who this stranger was, could he have been an angel or a divine messenger of some sort sent by God at a time when we needed it most? We don't know, but what we do know, is that God's timing is perfect and we are spiritually enriched by these personal experiences, recalling the words of our Lord, "I will never leave thee nor forsake thee." When we went to see James soon after the stranger had gone his condition gave no cause for concern. We have one word to describe it...miraculous.

BE NOT FORGETFUL TO ENTERTAIN STRANGERS: FOR THEREBY SOME HAVE ENTERTAINED ANGELS UNAWARES.

HEBREWS 13 v 2

CHAPTER 18

Two Hours to Live

Despite our best efforts, it was impossible to get a sufficient amount of sleep during those first few days. We were unable to clear our minds, even for a short time, to allow us to get over to sleep. Our minds were filled with thoughts and questions about James growing up, his whole life would flash in front of us, not to mention my own life and where did I go wrong for all this to happen to any child of mine. What did I ever do that God should allow this to happen, was this my entire fault? Yes it is so easy to blame yourself when things go wrong and as always the one question we always came back to..WHY? Well we would struggle on attempting to show a brave face for the sake of others. We were five days in and all was well, or so we thought.

After tea time relatives and friends started to arrive at the hospital. Then soon after this we were taken to yet another private room by a sister from I.C.U. We were asked to sit down as the Neurosurgeon wanted to speak to us. The mood changed and everyone became very sombre as it was obvious that we were being prepared to be told bad news. Our hearts sank and the blood drained from our faces. The news was for Jennifer and me only. We were told to make sure that some family members were close by. What on earth were we going to hear?

The Surgeon came into the room and sat down. He started to explain that things had taken a turn for the worse. There was a massive deterioration in our son's condition and his brain pressure had increased to such an extent that he was dangerously close to death. There was now no possibility of surgical intervention and it was explained that a hole could

Two Hours to Live

not be drilled into his head to relieve the pressure. The other option had been to remove a brain flap by taking away part of his skull; surgically implanting it in his stomach until the brain pressure returned to normal, again this was now not possible. James' brain pressure should have been below 20 on the monitor, but was now reading 43, in short, there was nothing else they could do. They gave James two hours to live and told us it was now time to get all the family together to say our final farewells.

We were stunned into disbelief and then Jennifer became inconsolable, I pleaded with the doctor to do something but he shook his head. We cried out to the doctor to help but he said, "I am sorry, there is nothing I can do, it is only a matter of time now." I said to the surgeon, "No, he is not going to die and my God is going to make an idiot out of you." With that, the meeting ended.

We then had to inform the family members already there and contact those who had not yet arrived as we attempted to get everyone in to see James and said their goodbyes. The hospital waiting room became like a morgue as everyone was stunned into a macabre silence before the wave of uncontrollable crying and disbelief descended. Jennifer and I were the first to go in to see James as he lay helpless in the Intensive Care Unit. Our eyes were drawn to the brain monitor, which told its own story. His brain pressure was now reading 50 and we just knew his life was hanging in the balance, suspended between earth and Heaven. I thought this could not be happening, after all God had told me not to doubt so why should we be told by the doctors he was going to die? All we wanted was our son alive and well, but it is at times like this that all sorts of thoughts go through your head and what I was thinking in my time of desperation was can I do a deal with God? What if I was to die instead of James? I wished with all my heart that it was me lying there at death's door instead of my son. After all, James had his life in front of him. These were only momentary and I soon snapped out of it, realising that you don't do deals with the Almighty God no matter what. One thing is certain; I would gladly have given my life in exchange for his.

The situation got even worse when we brought James' sister and brother, Naomi and Philip in to say goodbye. Philip stood at the side of the bed holding James' hand, just breaking his young heart. I remember thinking that no child should ever have to go through this. Then Naomi became hysterical as she lay across James, screaming and crying and pleading with God not to let her brother die. This was the most heartbreaking moment I have ever experienced it was unreal and I think, at that time, we all wanted to die as we could not bear the pain of losing him. Family members came and went, then some close friends; everyone was crying, everyone was devastated. Prayers were sent to heaven that night like never before and without ceasing, with floods of tears. I don't do crying, not ever, but that night the tears of a lifetime cried out to Almighty God to save my son; I had never known so much pain or sorrow.

Everyone was reluctant to leave, but they all eventually went home as there was nothing anyone could do. That night both Jennifer and I died a little bit as we sat at our son's bedside at 3 am in a private room in the Intensive Care Unit, seemingly all alone to any on-lookers, but very much aware of the presence of God. So in our devastated and completely broken state and unable to function properly, Jennifer and I prayed the prayer to end all prayers;

"God, we know that James is really your child and not ours, because we are all your children and so if you decide to take James home to be with you in glory, then we now surrenderhim into Your hands and we will accept Your decision without question BUT we love him and we don't want to give him up just yet, so we now claim him back and ask you to give him back to us no matter how he ends up we want him back, we ask this in Jesus' name and we claim Your promise that whatsoever we ask in Your name, believing we shall receive. Amen."

Two Hours to Live

We both experienced real peace as we were so aware of God's presence, we looked around for angels. The brain monitor now read a pressure of 53, and we knew that James should be dead, but he still clung to life.

On the morning of the sixth day, we were again told that James had not long to go before he would die and it was now time to give some consideration to donating his organs, this was something we had never considered until now. Later that morning, our pastor, David Dunlop, called with us and after explaining the situation to him, we discussed funeral arrangements with him should James die. At that time, our church was having building work carried out and we would need to make alternative arrangements for a church that could accommodate some 500 people or more. At this point David just stood and cried with us and our seemingly hopeless situation. We prayed with David that the situation would change and that James would be healed. We prayed long and hard until James' brain pressure dropped and we watched in awe as it fell to below 20. By late afternoon, the brain monitor was now reading 3, this was the miracle we had prayed for and although not out of the woods yet, James was out of danger; praise God.

This night was now so completely different from the night before and we could not contain our joy, everyone had seen a miracle from God. Desi and Elma Stafford then arrived at the hospital after having spent most of the previous night with us. Desi told us that when he got home, he pleaded with God to save James and to give him some sign of conformation, a word or something to encourage us, then he handed us a hand written note with an answer from God, it read;

"How blessed is he who considers the helpers,
The Lord will deliver him in a day of trouble.
The Lord will protect him and keep him alive,
The Lord will sustain him upon his sick bed
In his illness, thou dost restore him to health.

Psalm 41vv 1-3 ASV.

CHAPTER 19

Testing Times - Adele

James continued to make very slow but steady progress and before long he was well enough to be transferred to the Regional Acquired Brain Injury Unit at Musgrave Park Hospital in Belfast. There he would spend many months in rehabilitation and it was there he spent his eighteenth birthday. We, as a family struggled greatly in an effort to come to terms with what happened to James, often asking God the question why? We got no answer, but it was God alone who strengthened and comforted us through those dark days.

ADELE
Unfortunately, we were dealt another catastrophic blow, for only eleven weeks after James' accident, which had left our entire family circle devastated we received a telephone call around 3.00am on Saturday 15 September 2007 informing us that James' 14 year old cousin Adele had been knocked down and killed. Adele, had been coming home from a wedding when she was hit by a car on, Finaghy Road South, Belfast. This had become far too much to bear for a family already devastated beyond belief. What was left of our hearts was now completely crushed and broken.

Once again we had more questions, why had Adele been taken and James saved. No matter how hard we searched for answers, we found none. Our only comfort was that we believe that Adele went to be with the Lord. Remember, God never makes any mistakes.

THE LORDS PRAYER
Our Father which art in heaven, Hallowed be thy name.

Thy kingdom come. "Thy, will be done in earth." as it is in heaven.
Give us this day our daily bread.
And forgive us our debts, as we forgive our debtors.
And lead us not into temptation, but deliver us from evil:
For thine is the kingdom, and the power, and the glory,
For ever. AMEN

CHAPTER 20

James – Today

James came home from hospital in 2008 and at that time he was unable to sit unsupported, he was unable to walk and was wheelchair bound. James was paralysed down his right side. He was unable to feed himself nor able to control and handle toilet issues. James could not speak one word as a result of the accident and was now suffering from severe epileptic seizures, all of which did not make his long term prognosis good. We were told that there was nothing more that the doctors could do for him, but God had certainly not finished His divine work of healing.

Today James can walk with the aid of a walking stick. He can now engage in conversation. He can eat by himself and can attend to most of his toiletry needs himself. I believe that God used the doctors to do as much as they could, but after that, God continues to heal according to sovereign His will, which will always have ultimate good for those He loves.

IF I MAY TOUCH BUT HIS CLOTHES, I SHALL BE WHOLE.

MARK 5 v 28 KJV

CHAPTER 21

Why Me Lord?

For many years I have pondered that very question, Why, Me Lord? Why, has my life taken this particular course? Why, did I experience the most unbelievable situations of extreme, danger? Why, did I have such a constant battle against the forces of evil most of my adult life? While I accept that this has been the plan of God for my life, I believe that now is the time for me to relate some of my experiences from my journey through life. It is my prayer, you will receive blessing and encouragement from an awesome God, who remains the same, yesterday, today and forever.

GOD HAS ENCOURAGED ME WITH THESE WORDS:

BUT I WANT YOU TO KNOW, BRETHREN,
THAT THE THINGS THAT HAPPENED TO ME
HAVE ACTUALLY TURNED OUT FOR THE
FURTHERANCE OF THE GOSPEL.

PHILIPPIANS 1 v 12

WHY ME LORD?

TELL ME LORD IF YOU THINK THERE'S A WAY,
I CAN TRY TO REPAY ALL I'VE TAKEN FROM YOU.
MAYBE LORD I CAN SHOW SOMEONE ELSE,
WHAT I'VE BEEN THROUGH MYSELF, ON MY WAY BACK TO YOU.

(KRISTOFFERSON)